The
Social
Visionary

*The Dynamics of
Social Leadership*

Andre Thomas

GREATNESS
PUBLISHING

www.ideasandsolutions.org

Cover Design and formatting by Farouk J. Roberts,
Brands & Love Creative
www.brandsnlove.com

Library and Archives Canada
ISBN: 978-1-927579-08-4

Dedication

I dedicate this book to the social entrepreneurs in Barbados and the wider Caribbean who work night and day behind the scenes to add value to the marginalized groups in our region. I learnt many lessons about social entrepreneurial leadership while working with you.

Acknowledgements

I wish to thank my wife Nina Thomas for typing out this manuscript.

Farouk J. Roberts for his skill in formatting and design. and Valentine Dantes for his editorial work.

Contents

The
Social
Entrepreneur

Chapter One

ARE YOU A SOCIAL ENTREPRENEUR?

Any nation that is weak in grooming indigenous social entrepreneurs would be an emotionally cold place to live in.

Who is a social entrepreneur? I define a social entrepreneur as a visionary leader who brings large-scale systemic and sustainable social change through innovation, new processes, application of existing technologies and strategy or a combination of these. His or her focus is not on profit margins, but on creating social transformation for poor or marginalized groups in a financially sustainable way.

The genetic gift in social entrepreneurs equips them to apply practical, innovative and sustainable approaches that benefit society on a whole with an emphasis on the marginalized and poor. Their approach to solving economic and social problems cuts across sectors and disciplines. They are empowered by their strong social conscience and are driven by their values, whether the focus is education, health, welfare reform, human rights, workers rights, environment, economic developments or agriculture.

The organization they lead could be non-profit or for profit entities. However, it is the leveraging of innovation, human skills, material and financial resources for a social transformation mission, which makes an authentic social entrepreneur a gift to every community. They occupy a unique space between those who work purely in charities and depend on charity and the entrepreneur who creates goods and services that add value to people for a profit. The social entrepreneur has his feet planted in both camps. His vision and mission are social, yet he will use entrepreneurial approaches to achieve them.

Social entrepreneurs have created some of the greatest organizations that span the medical world, human rights, immigrants' rights, child welfare, educational, people empowerment, environmental, disaster relief and poverty alleviation. Social entrepreneurs see the social needs gap within communities that government and society are not meeting and take the necessary steps to create innovative products, inspire people, and marshal financial resources to meet them. In other words, they fill the social gaps left by government and society with workable transformational solutions.

Traits of a well-developed Social Entrepreneurship Gift

Just as it takes a genetic gift to be a successful business entrepreneur, so it is with social entrepreneurship. From my studies and research, I have discovered the following traits of social entrepreneurs:

1. Have a great social conscience

Social conscience can be defined as an attitude of sensitivity and responsibility regarding justice and problems in society. It is this trait that propels the social entrepreneur to engage in social change work.

On a scale of one to ten, with one being the least and ten being the highest, state your level of social consciousness.

1	2	3	4	5	6	7	8	9	10

2. Innovation

Innovation is thinking outside the box of history to apply new solutions to old problems. Social entrepreneurs excel in this trait because they challenge the status quo and come up with new and better solutions to address social or environmental problems. This trait empowers them to shrug off all restraints whether it is related to specific ideologies, disciplines or culture.

On a scale of one to ten, with one being the least and ten being the highest, state your level of innovation.

1	2	3	4	5	6	7	8	9	10

3. Solution Orientated

This trait enables social entrepreneurs to create social change with limited resources through their innovation and creativity. They are totally results-oriented and tend to use disruptive and innovative solutions, as well as unconventional and traditional ideas to solve problems.

On a scale of one to ten, with one being the least and ten being the highest, state your level of strength in creating or sourcing solutions for social problems you are passionate about.

1	2	3	4	5	6	7	8	9	10

4. Self-Confidence

Social entrepreneurship is certainly not a haven for the insecure. Trail blazing and being a change agent will certainly test your self-belief. Confidence is the bold expression of your authentic gifts, ideas, persona, vision and thoughts to others. Arrogance is an exaggerated expression of your gifts, ideas, persona, vision and thoughts to others and it's basically a lie. True social entrepreneurs are confident enough to swim upstream if required, as they bring social change through their innovative ideas, passion and gifts.

On a scale of one to ten, with one being the least and ten being the highest, state your level of self-confidence.

1	2	3	4	5	6	7	8	9	10

5. Passion

Passion is desire at boiling point. It is this boiling desire for social change that propels the social entrepreneur into action and sets him or her apart from mere social commentators.

On a scale of one to ten, with one being the least and ten being the highest, state your level of passion.

1	2	3	4	5	6	7	8	9	10

6. Good Communication Skills

This trait enables the social entrepreneur to inspire people through communication to help them with their enterprise. They are good at motivating and verbally detonating the skills and passions of people to accomplish their social visions.

On a scale of one to ten, with one being the least and ten being the highest, state your level of communication ability.

1	2	3	4	5	6	7	8	9	10

7. Organizational Leadership

All well-run organizations, manage human, financial and material resources in a structured and strategic way to accomplish predetermined objectives. Social entrepreneurs are endowed with organizational leadership strengths to enable them to organize human, financial and material resources to affect social change.

On a scale of one to ten, with one being the least and ten being the highest, state your level of competence in organizational leadership.

1	2	3	4	5	6	7	8	9	10

8. Adaptation

Most successful programs do not look exactly the way they were originally conceptualized. This is because, along the way, the social entrepreneur has had to alter the product, service or program based on the realities in the field. This ability to adapt and self-correct is a hallmark of great social entrepreneurs.

On a scale of one to ten, with one being the least and ten being the highest, state your level of competence in adapting your products, services and programs to realities on field of action.

1	2	3	4	5	6	7	8	9	10

9. Resourcefulness

Resourceful people know how to make the most out of limited resources. Social entrepreneurs have a knack for taking limited human, financial and material resources along with their expertise and influence, to make a gigantic social impact.

On a scale of one to ten, with one being the least and ten being the highest, state your level of innovation.

1	2	3	4	5	6	7	8	9	10

10. Team Builders

Social change is definitely a team effort and successful social entrepreneurs excel in the craft of team building. They build teams that include staff, partners, investors and grant donors, and unite them around their goals and objectives.

On a scale of one to ten, with one being the least and ten being the highest, state your level of team building.

1	2	3	4	5	6	7	8	9	10

11. Tenacity

Successful social entrepreneurs don't give up. For them, social transformation is not a sprint; it is a marathon. The story of William Wilberforce, the famous social reformer from Great Britain who fought slavery in the British colonies, illustrates this truth.

On a scale of one to ten, with one being the least and ten being the highest, state your level of tenacity.

1	2	3	4	5	6	7	8	9	10

12. Opportunity Hunters

Social entrepreneurs tend to be opportunity hunters. They are quick to spot and exploit opportunities that others may overlook. They are not daunted by, "It has never been done before" or "We need more resources." They sense when the human desire for change intersects with innovative solutions and maximize the moment to make social change, a reality.

On a scale of one to ten, with one being the least and ten being the highest, state your level of competence in opportunity hunting.

1	2	3	4	5	6	7	8	9	10

Your Social Entrepreneurial Score Card

Draw a circle around the number that best describes the strength of the various attributes of your social entrepreneurial gift. It is important that you are totally honest with yourself and if you need another opinion, ask someone close to you who will tell you the truth no matter what.

To find your average score, which will reveal the strength of your social entrepreneurial gift, add your score in each of the twelve categories and divide the sum by twelve.

The highest possible score will be 10, which is 120 divided by 12. A person with a strong social entrepreneurial gift will have an average score between 7 and 10. A person with a medium social entrepreneurial gift will score an average of 6.

What is your score? ☐

Programs and Products

Chapter Two

THE SOCIAL CHANGE MODEL

Successful social entrepreneurs only create a social change prescription after an accurate diagnosis of the social issues they are attempting to solve.

A social change model is what makes an organization a social venture organization. It is how it strategically delivers its social change prescription.

Diagnosing the problem and prescribing the social prescription

There are some distinct similarities between successful social entrepreneurs and effective medical doctors. Interestingly, there are also distinct similarities between unsuccessful social entrepreneurs and ineffective medical doctors.

Let's examine them in more details:

Similarities between successful social entrepreneurs and effective medical doctors:

Tasks	Effective Doctors	Successful Social Entrepreneurs
Diagnosis of Condition	They are committed to diagnose the medical condition using all avenues available to them before creating a prescription.	They are committed to diagnose the true nature of the negative social condition, before creating a social change prescription.
Context of Condition	They are committed to understand the context that created the condition in the patient and they use that knowledge to influence their prescription.	They are committed to thoroughly understand the context in which the social problem was created and they use that knowledge to create the social change prescription.
Consultation	They are committed to consult with other medical specialists where necessary before making a prescription.	They are committed to consult with stakeholders before prescribing and executing the social change prescription.
Assumptions	They are committed to examine and articulate the assumptions behind the prescriptions.	They are committed to examine and communicate the assumptions behind the social change prescriptions.
Evaluating goals and outcomes	They are committed to set specific measurable goals for their patients during treatments and measure the outcome to determine the success	They are committed to set specific goals for the social interventions and evaluate the

	ratio.	outcomes to determine their level of (SROI) social return on investments.

Similarities between ineffective doctors and unsuccessful social entrepreneurs:

Tasks	Ineffective Doctors	Unsuccessful Social Entrepreneurs
Diagnosis of Condition	They prescribe their favorite prescription for patients after hearing the patients' views on the conditions and do not examine the patients thoroughly.	They ignore the realities on the ground and always prescribe their favorite social change prescription as the answer.
Context of Condition	They do not ask the right questions to detect the context that created the condition.	They do not conduct a thorough research of the context that created the negative social condition.
Consultation	They are legends in their minds and only consult their brains before making prescriptions.	They ignore the potential contribution of other stakeholders and do it their way.
Assumptions	They do not articulate a cause and effect logic for their prescriptions.	Their assumptions are not gleaned from research but from their uninformed opinions.
Evaluating goals and outcomes	In their minds, their job is to try to help the patient but they do not follow a rigorous procedure of setting goals and evaluating treatment outcomes.	They are more excited about executing their pet projects than on the tangible social return on investment (SROI).

Wise social entrepreneurs focus on asking themselves and their teams the following diagnostic questions before prescribing and executing a social change solution.

Use the below questions as a framework to evaluate your social change project:

1. Who is experiencing the problem?

_____

_____

_____

_____

_____

_____

_____

2. What is the problem?

_____

_____

_____

_____

_____

_____

_____

3. What is the scale of the problem?

_____

_____

_____

_____

_____

_____

_____

4. What would become of the condition if the problem were solved?

_____

_____

_____

_____

_____

_____

_____

5. What is the root cause of the problem?

_____

_____

_____

_____

_____

_____

_____

6. Have there been any attempts to solve the problem and if so, why have they been unsuccessful?

_____

_____

_____

_____

_____

_____

_____

7. Are there any other social change entities seeking to solve the problem?

_____

_____

_____

_____

_____

_____

_____

Creating the social change prescription

In creating the social change prescription, there are three critical phases of the project that must be clearly defined:

1. Define Current State of The Problem

At this stage, you utilize all the wisdom gleaned from doing a 360-degree diagnosis of the problem by using the questions in the earlier section.

2. Define The Desired State of The Problem

This process might seem obvious, but from my experience many social entrepreneurs fail to clearly divine the specific, measureable, achievable, realistic and time-bound (SMART), outcomes that their efforts are designed to achieve.

3. Define The Social Change Actions That Will Be Utilized To Bring About The Desired State of The Problem

This process involves the social entrepreneur defining the core interventions that will be utilized along with the supporting assumptions that undergird its potential for success. In addition, the supporting actions that are required to undergird the core interventions must be defined.

An example of strategic thinking for social entrepreneurs:
The Social Problem

The Compton Towers community also known as the Carnal Towers, has just exploded in violence over the last three months. Four teenagers were found dead in a dilapidated building, killed in execution style. The local government in response has setup a taskforce to tackle this upsurge in violence and bring economic empowerment to the community. A dynamic experienced and strategic social entrepreneur was appointed to lead the taskforce.

The Social Diagnosis

The taskforce decided to engage in a comprehensive 360-degree analysis of the root cause of the problem before rushing in to make a social change prescription. This process took place in tandem with the deployment of additional police officers in the community to bring about an induced calmness, while a prescription was being developed.

After a month of extensive research including interviews with residents and other stakeholders, the team arrived at the following conclusions:

The Problem

Eighty percent of youth in the Compton community are not actively parented and are low achievers in school.

The Fruit of The Problem

There are about four hundred teenagers who roam about aimlessly without parental supervision and a clear vision for tomorrow and who are also being recruited by drug, prostitution and criminal gangs to work for them.

The Context of The Problem

Compton Towers was a low cost government housing project where single and teenage mothers were given government housing. These mothers did not change their financial and parenting philosophy when they moved into the housing project. Instead, they continued having unplanned babies, relying on the state to parent their children and being dependent on using their bodies to create formal or informal income for themselves, hence the reason for its unofficial name "Carnal Towers."

The Outcome of Other Social Change Interventions

All other social change interventions did not bring real change to the community due to the fact that they did not transform the paradigms, philosophies and earning power of the residents. Most of the interventions consisted of sports, food and clothing assistance programs just to name a few. These only brought cosmetic change and had not tackled the core issues of unplanned pregnancies, poor parenting and systemic poverty thinking.

The Current State of The Problem

The Compton Towers community is now a breeding ground for commercial sex workers, drug gangs and other criminal gangs. It also had a teenage pregnancy and youth incarceration culture. Sixty percent of all drug, criminal and commercial sex activities in the town can be traced to Compton Towers.

The Desired State of The Problem

That the Compton Towers community will become a thriving, working, economic class community that produces children who add value to the nation.

Core Social Change Interventions

1. Create a favorable economic zone within the community's area in the form of an industrial park for manufacturing companies like dressmakers, furniture manufactures, paint manufactures and canned food manufactures. The companies operating within the business park will be given a low local tax as well as low customs and excise taxes. In return, they would be required to employ at least fifty percent of their workforce from the Compton Towers community.

2. Include leadership development as a subject in the local primary and secondary school for all students.

3. Create a six-week parenting class within the community and upon completion, give each participant a three hundred dollar food voucher for shopping at the local food bank. This would evidently have to result in a change of policy as mothers within the community have already developed a habit of just

going to the food bank and taking food. Now, it will be food only on the basis that you would make yourself available to sit in the six-week parenting class.

4.   To make commercial space available at low cost to proven morality development organizations like churches, youth and men and women empowerment organizations. An accountability system will be created which will ensure that preferential leases to these organizations would be evaluated annually based on their social return.

5.   A small office will be created within the community to facilitate and oversee the four-year social change program.

Core Supporting Actions

1.   To secure local government approval for the transformation of the local business park to an economic zone that would directly benefit Compton Towers. This policy will end the practice of wealth companies benefiting from low commercial rent on the border of a poor community. The rational is that these affluent organizations can pay more expensive rent in other upscale parts of town and if they wanted to stay and benefit from the low costs of land and commercial space beside Compton Towers, they would have to make a valuable contribution.

2.   To have a town hall style meeting once approval has been given to provide information to the companies, churches and social organizations that want to seize the twin opportunity of advancing the agenda and positively transforming Compton Towers at the same time.

3.   To identify a leadership curriculum development company that will help integrate the new school subject into the school system at Compton Towers.

4.   To recruit administrative social staff to execute the five-year Compton Towers social change plan.

5.   To recruit a team of parenting coaches that would conduct the parenting classes.

6.   To create a food voucher system at the local food bank.

Strategic questions that must be answered before creating a social change prescription:

What is the current state of the problem?

_____

_____

_____

_____

_____

_____

_____

_____

What is the desired state of the problem?

_____

_____

_____

_____

_____

_____

_____

List the core interventions that will be utilized to bring about change from the current state to the desired state?

_____

_____

_____

_____

_____

_____

_____

_____

_____

_____

_____

_____

_____

_____

List the supporting actions that are necessary to undergird the core interventions?

_____

_____

_____

_____

_____

_____

_____

_____

_____

_____

_____

_____

_____

The
Social
Venture

Chapter Three

ORGANIZING TO EXECUTE YOUR SOCIAL VENTURE

A great social change idea executed by a passionate disorganized group of people will lead to failure

The organizing of human capitals, materials and financial capital in a structured and strategic way to execute predefined social change objectives is the lifeblood of every successful social venture. Many emerging entrepreneurs, when they dream about social change, often do not totally count the cost of what is required to successfully turn the social change idea into reality. The development of a well-run organization is usually one of the issues that are overlooked.

In my many years of working with sincere and authentic visionary social entrepreneurs, I have discovered that seventy five percent percent of them fail to maximize the impact of their vision. This is because they fail to strategically build an efficient organization to execute the vision. They score high on authenticity, vision, drive and self-belief, but score very poorly on strategy, organization development and execution. In this chapter I am going to share the principles that any authentic social entrepreneur can use to begin building an efficient, dynamic organization that delivers the social change it promises.

Foundational Principles For Building A Social Venture Organization

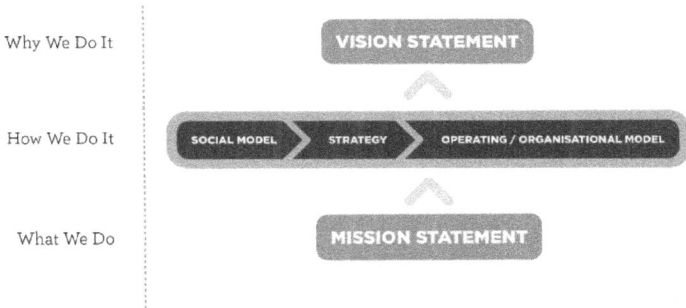

Why We Do It — VISION STATEMENT

How We Do It — SOCIAL MODEL > STRATEGY > OPERATING / ORGANISATIONAL MODEL

What We Do — MISSION STATEMENT

I will use examples of social organizations that I have done consultancy for and The Ideas and Solutions Group (a social venture organization that I lead) to illustrate the application of these principles:

No two organizations can authentically be the same, as they will have different organizational DNA. Authentic visions are as unique as fingerprints; each one is different, so use the example of my organization to inspire you to structure your venture for success.

The organizational model of your venture must not be a secret as people tend to support what they understand and believe in.

Principle Number 1

Vision

The vision of an organization is a clear mental portrait of why the organization was created and the problem it is designed to solve.

Example:

Our Vision for The Ideas and Solutions Group is to see a global movement of the 12 types of leaders that shape the destiny of nations emerge and take their ideas and solutions from concept to reality.

Principle Number 2

The Social Change Model

The social change model of your organization is the strategic way it has chosen to deliver social change.

Principle Number 3

Strategy

Strategy is a series of sequential steps that takes you from your current reality to a predefined future by domino effect. All good strategy includes these three foundational pillars:

A. A brutally honest assessment of current reality.

B. A clear definition of the shape of the future that can be possessed based on the potential of the present.

C. Supporting assumptions that undergird the sequential steps in your strategic plan.

Principle Number 4

Core Interventions and Supporting Actions

An efficient social entrepreneurial organization predefines and makes clear its core social interventions and supporting operational actions. This clarity empowers its staff and partners to intelligently run with the vision.

Principle Number 5

Operating / Organizational Model

Efficient social entrepreneur organizations systemize their core interventions and support actions into an operating system.

Principle Number 6

Organizational Structure

The structure of an organization determines how it behaves.

Principle Number 7

High impact social organizations are structured for efficiency rather than bureaucracy.

Example of The Ideas and Solutions Group:

Our organization is broken down into three entities:

> *Greatness Publishing* - publishes leadership development and greatness empowerment books. These books are at the foundation of our social change prescription.

1. *Igniting World Changers* - which is an executive leadership coaching, organizational development and strategy consulting organization.

2. *University of Innovation and Leadership* – This is a conference and seminar organization that conducts

events globally around the themes of innovation and leadership.

Example of the organizational structure of the Compton Towers development corporation
Chairman and CEO

- Responsible for the strategic direction of the organization

- Responsible for the strategic oversight of the organization

- Responsible for leading the corporate board

- Responsible for initiating and managing strategic partnership for the advancement of the organization mission

- Responsible for ensuring that the organization functions out of it's predefine core cultural values

- Responsible for ensuring that the five-year development plan is executed in its totality

Chief Operating Officer

- Responsible for the day-to-day running of the organization

- Responsible for ensuring that all team members execute their operational tasks

- Responsible for evaluating and reporting the monthly outcomes of core interventions to the CEO and board

Chief Financial Officer

- Responsible for managing the finances of the corporation to achieve its strategic objectives

- Responsible for creating budgets and financial requests to local government

- Responsible for ensuring that all statutory financial and good accounting practices are met

- Responsible for measuring the social return on investment

- Responsible for negotiating and signing the leases with tenants

Office Manager

- Responsible for managing the workload of the social intervention officers

- Responsible for managing the day-to-day operations of the office

- Responsible for providing a vacancy information service for residents

- Responsible for providing a job recruitment service for commercial tenants

Social Interventions Officers

- Responsible for recruiting and signing people up for the corporations programs and services

- Responsible for matching job seekers with vacancies in the Compton Towers business estate

- Responsible for teaching at the parenting class

- Responsible for providing general counseling to residents

As you may observe, this is a very clear outline of the responsibilities, duties and tasks of the Compton Towers development corporation. These responsibilities cover all the core interventions and support actions required to execute the social change model.

Principle Number 8

Mission

The mission of an organization is what its focus should be on a daily basis to accomplish its vision.

Example:

The mission of The Ideas and Solutions Group is to create a leadership wisdom culture in nations through strategic partnerships, publications, leadership coaching, strategy consulting, organizational development, leadership empowerment events, media and youth empowerment.

Financing The Vision

Chapter Four

FINANCING THE SOCIAL VENTURE

Money is the fuel of dreams

To the novice social entrepreneur, obtaining the finance is more important than defining the vision, social model, strategy, organizational model, operating model and mission. They tend to convince themselves that all they need to do is to get the money and then later figure out what to do with it.

In the real world, except you are self-financing the entire social venture vision, you will be found guilty of putting the cart before the horse. One of the first laws that you must understand about raising money for projects is that people are more willing to buy into a vision they believe in. This applies to friends, family, grant agencies, government agencies, banks and venture capital companies.

The Social Venture Blueprint

It then follows, that in order to persuade people to invest in your social venture vision, you must take the time to:

1.   Define the social venture vision

2.   Thoroughly research your social change model.

3.   Craft a well thought out strategy

4.   Create an operating model that will deliver results

5.   Define an organizational model that maximizes the potential of your team

6.   Construct a clear mission statement that will guide your daily operations and protect your focus

When the above is in place, you have what I call: *The Social Venture Blueprint* that you can now submit to friends, family, grant agencies, government agencies, equity partners, banks and venture capital companies etc.

The Legal Structure of Your Social Venture

The legal structure of your social venture will determine the type of investment you can receive into your vision and therefore, must be well thought-out.

Two examples of this would be:

A.   A Social Venture grant agency will typically not invest in a for profit company with a social mission.

B.   A Social Venture with the legal structure of a charity will be unable to receive equity finance as it cannot issue shares and disburse profits.

It is important that you research the various legal structures in your nation that social enterprises can utilize, and then choose the vehicle that optimizes your social venture blueprint.

I will use the example of the United Kingdom's legal vehicle options for social enterprises as their laws have being duplicated in many nations.

FINANCING THE SOCIAL VENTURE

LEGAL STRUCTURE	KEY FEATURES	PROS	CONS
Unincorporated Association (Voluntary / Community Organisations)			
Registered Charity (unincorporated association)			
Company Limited by Guarantee			
Registered Charity (company limited by guarantee)			
Company Limited by Shares			
Industrial & Provident Society			
Community Interest Company (CIC)			

Funding Sources

There are many different funding options that different entrepreneurs can use to fuel their social venture vision.

1. Self-Financing

This involves the social entrepreneur using his own assets and capital to fund the start-up and/or operational expenses of the venture.

2. Relational Financing

In this option, the social entrepreneur receives funding from friends, family and close acquaintances to fuel the start-up and/or operational expenses of the venture. This funding may come in the form of financial gifts, loans or pro bono services.

3. Products Financing

When it comes to product financing, the social enterprise produces goods and/or services that add value to people at a profit and then turn around and use the profit to fuel the social vision.

4. Grant Financing

This involves the social enterprise receiving a grant from an agency from which there is no repayment that is tied to a particular project, accountability and performance indicators.

5. Equity Financing

This involves the social enterprise receiving funding from equity partners who will gain shares in return and be entitled to a percentage of the profits produced by the venture. The profits that are not disbursed to equity partners are then used to fuel the growth of the venture.

In this model, the equity partners may not have rights to influence the strategic direction of the venture.

6. Debt Financing

In debt financing, the social enterprise obtains the loan from a lending institution at a payment rate it can afford to fuel the social venture vision. Debt financing may be use for startup capital, operating expenses or growth opportunities.

7. Mass Small Donor Financing

In this option, the social entrepreneur shares the vision with certain sections of the public in a way and manner that inspires him or her to give regular small donations to the venture in a formal way. The small donations can be given through a credit card, direct debit, cash or cheque payments, and monthly or yearly statements of a provided to the small donors for tax purposes if required.

8. Hybrid Models

Many social enterprises use a combination of the above sources of finances to fuel their vision. At the Ideas and

Comment [VD]: Not sure what's supposed to go there but something doesn't sound right

Solutions Group we use self-financing, product financing and grant financing.

Managing The Finance

Money is the fuel of dreams and therefore, it must be managed. Drivers instinctively manage the fuel in their tank. They don't go to bed and leave the car on while they sleep because they can. They intuitively understand that doing that is a useless exercise that would empty their fuel tank. This same principle applies to money.

When social enterprises or any organization do not carefully manage their money, they can hemorrhage finances on activities as useless as leaving a car on at night till morning. Similarly, there are certain projects that will empty out your tank and eventually hinder you from progress. Money must not be wasted regardless of how much money a person has.

I have included a financial management diagram to help social entrepreneurs ask the right questions that would help them manage the resources they have.

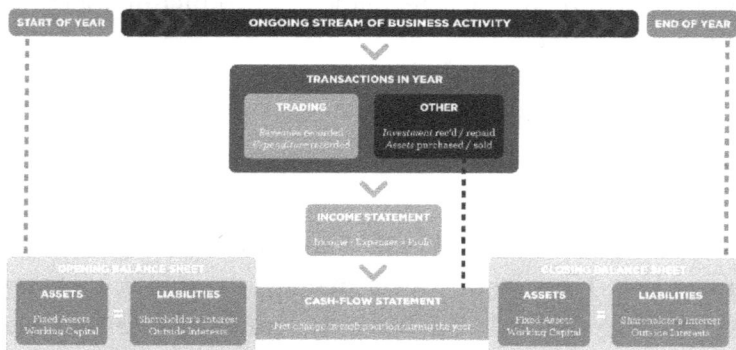

START OF YEAR

ONGOING STREAM OF BUSINESS ACTIVITY

END OF YEAR

TRANSACTIONS IN YEAR

TRADING
Revenues received
Expenditure incurred

OTHER
Investment rec'd / repaid
Assets purchased / sold

INCOME STATEMENT
Income - Expenses = Profit

OPENING BALANCE SHEET

ASSETS		LIABILITIES
Fixed Assets Working Capital	=	Shareholder's Interest Outside Interests

CASH-FLOW STATEMENT
Net change in cash position during the year

CLOSING BALANCE SHEET

ASSETS		LIABILITIES
Fixed Assets Working Capital	=	Shareholder's Interest Outside Interests

Executing The Vision

Chapter Five

IT TAKES A LEADER TO MAKE THE VISION HAPPEN

If the leadership wisdom in the visionary does not match the vision, the vision will become the object of the visionary's frustration.

Leadership wisdom is the raw material for the fulfillment of vision. Wisdom is thinking thoughts, applying principles and taking steps to create what you desire.

Leadership is using influence to work with and through people to accomplish a vision. It is possible to have an authentic vision that you can possess in the future that is currently greater than your leadership capacity. In that case, what is required is growth. A practical example of this was demonstrated when I saw my young three-year old daughter attempt to take the house keys from the dining table. She could see the keys, but the height of the table was beyond her reach. I could not help but think that one day when she grows up, she would not only be able to walk to the dining table and take the keys with ease, but she would also have her own keys to the house. This is the picture of the power of growth.

Potential can be defined as what you can be, do and have if you submit to a growth process. I have no doubt that within you is the ability to bring social change to your world of influence; otherwise, you wouldn't be reading this book. However, the non-negotiable price for the realization of your potential and the fulfillment of your dream is personal and leadership growth.

In this chapter, I am going to highlight areas that every social entrepreneur must seek to grow in, in order to fulfill his or her social and entrepreneurial potential.

1. Social Change Model Development

The social change model is the heart of every successful social enterprise. The process of developing a social change model is akin to the process of product development for a business entrepreneur. The ability and capacity to create an effective social change model is one that will require your personal growth through experience, study and mentorship.

2. Vision Casting

Social leaders shape the future with social change ideas that have become fully developed visions. These visions are the shape of the future that guides the social entrepreneurs day-to-day actions. Authentic vision is the ability to see a future that belongs to you and take steps everyday to align yourself to the manifestation of it. True vision is not a pipe dream. It is the pictures of what the future can be if you develop what you already have access to. It is the picture of the tomato fruit on a packet of tomato seeds. The vision of the fruit of a social venture never looks like the seed of the venture. Just like the tomato fruit looks very different from the tomato seed, so will your fully developed social enterprise look very different from your startup social venture. Vision casting is the skill of compellingly communicating your vision to those whose participation in its fulfillment is critical to its success.

One of the common mistakes that immature social visionaries make, is they focus on the features of the vision. Mature social visionaries do not do that. They focus on the problem the vision is designed to solve.

Your vision will have many features however, you must learn how to communicate it to your circle of success relationships.

These relationships include:

A. Board Members

They add value to your organization by bringing in their influence, talent and treasure to your success equation.

B. Funding Relationships

They financially invest in the social change vision.

C. Staff Team

They execute the vision on a daily basis

D. Government Agencies

They regulate and may partner with you in your efforts to bring about social change.

E. Media

They highlight the success or failure of your social change prescription.

F. Social Change Beneficiaries

These are the people that your social change services are designed to add value to.

3. Path-finding

True social enterprise leaders see beyond where the organization is and are constantly plotting out the best course to take to achieve the mission of the organization. Path-finding involves both strategic planning and tactical maneuvers. Strategy is a series of sequential synchronize steps to take you from your current reality to your desired future.

Good strategic planning always begins with a brutally honest definition of current reality. It then accurately discerns the possibility of the future and creates a path to get there using first, second and third order effect.

Tactical intelligence on the other hand, is the ability to quickly perceive a situation, evaluate multiple actions and take actions to get the desired results.

Great social entrepreneurs follow a well thought-out strategic plan, and in the heat of fast changing situations that affect them, make wise tactical decisions that cause them to win. The task of navigational leadership involves both tactics and strategy.

4. Creating Your Dream Team

The leadership of an organization will determine its rise or fall. The vision of an organization determines its focus and effectiveness. The structure of an organization will determine its behavior. The people within the organization determine its potential.

Excellent people are the potentially appreciating assets within organizations. Attracting diligent people who add value to your organization and putting them in the right place is indispensable to running a successful enterprise. The type of people you have in your organization matters. As the CEO, you are the chief cultural officer by default and it's in your best interest to create a culture that attracts, maintains and rewards excellence.

The dream team of many successful social enterprises tend to involve the use of volunteers who are not motivated by money, but by the reward of offering a service to a group of people. Your team building ability will determine whether

Comment [VD]: The word organizat[...] was used a bit too much in this paragraph your organization attracts and retains talents or if it's a revolving door.

5. Organizational Alignment

Management is the optimum stewardship of all existing resources to achieve objectives. Social entrepreneurial leaders though rich with human resources, material resources, financial assets and brand loyalty, can fail if they do not align these four elements in a structured and strategic way to achieve predetermined objectives.

6. Financing

The ability to attract the funding required to fuel the social venture is indispensable. Many great social ventures have run out of financial gas on the highway of real social transformation. Well-developed social entrepreneurs will usually find a way to secure funding for their social transformation dreams using everything at their disposal.

7. Financial Management

Becoming an expert on operating on a shoestring budget is part of social entrepreneurship. This involves management. My suggestion is that if you are not a good financial manager, you should hire one or find somebody within your circle of relations to manage the finances for you. This is important, as no amount of money will ever be enough for a poor financial manager. History has shown us that people have wasted fortunes that exceed half a billion dollars.

7. Modeling

The key question I ask social entrepreneurs on the subject of modeling and self-leadership is this: if the members of your team had your passion, integrity and competence will the social venture succeed or fail? Self-leadership is the ability to master yourself so that you bring the best out of yourself and not self-sabotage.

STOP AND REFLECT

On a scale on 1 to 10 assess your current level of strength in these leadership competences.

1. Social Change Model Development

1	2	3	4	5	6	7	8	9	10

2. Vision Casting

1	2	3	4	5	6	7	8	9	10

3. Path-finding

1	2	3	4	5	6	7	8	9	10

4. Creating Your Dream Team

1	2	3	4	5	6	7	8	9	10

5. Organizational Alignment

1	2	3	4	5	6	7	8	9	10

6. Financing

1	2	3	4	5	6	7	8	9	10

7. Financial Management

1	2	3	4	5	6	7	8	9	10

8. Modeling

1	2	3	4	5	6	7	8	9	10

Social entrepreneurs bring great value to the world. When they succeed, they always make the world a better place. To the social entrepreneurs reading this book, I encourage you to study your craft, seek mentorship, learn from your peers and pay the price of intentional growth. I believe you can do it and add value to the world.

About The Author

Andre Thomas is a Thought Leader, Author, Leadership Coach and Executive Strategy Consultant. He has worked as a Consultant for numerous organizations including: Government Agencies, Business Organizations and Social Organizations

He has conducted numerous seminars for the Private-sector, the United Nations (UN), Government and Non-governmental Agencies.

Thought Leader and Author

Andre Thomas is a Strategic Thinker on the subject of Leadership for The Transformation of Nations and a prolific author on the subject of leadership. His books include:

1.   The Organizational Visionary *(The Dynamics of Organizational Leadership)*
2.   The Gift of Political Leadership
3.   12 Spheres of Leadership *(The 12 Types of Leaders That Shape The Destinies Of Nations)*
4.   Unlock Your Greatness *(A Young Leaders' Handbook)*
5.   Discovering Me
6.   Uncommon Men and Distinguished Women

Leadership Coach

Andre Thomas is a Dynamic Leadership Coach that motivates and teaches the concepts and mechanics of leadership in a way that all ages and levels of society can understand. His seminars have included participants from Private, Social, Governmental and Non-Governmental Sectors.

Executive Strategy and Governance Consultant

Andre Thomas is a Gifted Executive Strategy Consultant with a wealth of experience in creating strategic solutions for leaders and organizational development solutions for organizations.

He is the founder and president of The Ideas and Solutions Group::A group of organizations that work through strategic partnerships, events, coaching, media, resources and consulting to create a leadership wisdom culture in organizations and nations that takes ideas and solutions from concept to reality.

Websites

www.ideasandsolutions.org

The Ideas And
Solutions Group

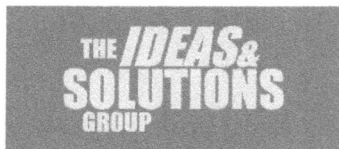

Purpose
To equip a critical mass of leaders in nations to bring ideas and solutions from concept to reality through the principles and process of transformational leadership and economic dignity

Vision
To see transformation occur in nations and their economies as leaders emerge to bring ideas and solutions from concept to reality.

Philosophy

1.   The problems of a generation will never be greater than the ideas and solutions within people born into that generation.
2.   These ideas and solutions are within people in the form of an uncommon vision.
3.   Leadership wisdom is applying principles and taking steps to take ideas and solutions from concept to reality.

4.   Except the leadership wisdom operating the visionary matches the scope of the vision, the uncommon vision within them will not be fulfilled.

<u>Other Books By</u>
<u>Greatness Publishing</u>

Nina D Thomas

1.   Woman, Get Off that Bus

Andre Thomas

1.   The Organizational Visionary   *(The Dynamics of Organizational Leadership)*
2.   The Gift of Political Leadership
3.   12 Spheres of Leadership *(The 12 Types of Leaders That Shape The Destinies Of Nations)*
4.   Unlock Your Greatness *(A Young Leaders' Handbook)*
5.   Discovering Me
6.   Uncommon Men and Distinguished Women
7.   Coaching People into the 12 Spheres of Leadership
8.   Seven Principles of Commonwealth Leadership
9.   Discovering your Leadership Assignment
10.   Preparing for your Leadership Assignment

To make bulk purchases email us at:

COO@IDEASANDSOLUTIONS.ORG